SERENA WILLIAMS
AND
ALEXIS OHANIAN

POWER COUPLES™

SERENA WILLIAMS AND ALEXIS OHANIAN

Alexis Burling

New York

Published in 2020 by The Rosen Publishing Group, Inc.
29 East 21st Street, New York, NY 10010

Copyright © 2020 by The Rosen Publishing Group, Inc.

First Edition

All rights reserved. No part of this book may be reproduced in any form without permission in writing from the publisher, except by a reviewer.

Library of Congress Cataloging-in-Publication Data

Names: Burling, Alexis, author.
Title: Serena Williams and Alexis Ohanian / Alexis Burling.
Description: First edition. | New York: Rosen Publishing, 2020. | Series: Power couples | Includes bibliographical references and index. | Audience: Grades 7–12.
Identifiers: LCCN 2018052186| ISBN 9781508188971 (library bound) | ISBN 9781508188964 (pbk.)
Subjects: LCSH: Williams, Serena, 1981- —Juvenile literature. | African American tennis players—Biography—Juvenile literature. | Women tennis players—United States—Biography—Juvenile literature. | Ohanian, Alexis, 1983- —Juvenile literature. | Businesspeople—United States—Biography—Juvenile literature. | Married people—United States—Biography—Juvenile literature.
Classification: LCC GV994.W55 B87 2020 | DDC 796.3420922 [B]—dc23
LC record available at https://lccn.loc.gov/2018052186

Manufactured in China

On the cover: On April 25, 2018, Serena Williams and Alexis Ohanian attend the New York premiere of the HBO documentary *Being Serena*.

CONTENTS

INTRODUCTION 6

CHAPTER 1
MADE FOR THE COURT 10

CHAPTER 2
INTERNET WHIZ KID 25

CHAPTER 3
A CHANCE ENCOUNTER 40

CHAPTER 4
THE YEAR OF CHANGE 51

CHAPTER 5
FULL-TIME PARENTS 65

CHAPTER 6
A MATCH MADE FOR WINNING 79

TIMELINE 90
GLOSSARY 93
FOR MORE INFORMATION 95
FOR FURTHER READING 99
BIBLIOGRAPHY 101
INDEX 108

INTRODUCTION

In November 2017, the world was watching as two of the most famous people in the United States came together as one. In front of an audience of hundreds of family members, friends, and fellow celebrities, Serena Williams and Alexis Ohanian got married in a lavish ceremony in New Orleans,

Serena Williams and Alexis Ohanian are one of the world's most beloved power couples. With fortune, fame, and undying love and respect for each other, these two seem to have it all.

INTRODUCTION

Louisiana. With their union now official, they solidified their status as America's latest supersonic power couple—two beloved and ultrasuccessful individuals whose lives together had the potential to become even greater than what either of them could accomplish apart.

But up until that point, both Williams and Ohanian had achieved plenty on their own. Williams began her professional career in tennis early, at age fourteen. By the time she was seventeen in 1999, she had won her first major title at the US Open. Over the next eighteen years, she played in four Olympics, winning four gold medals. She became one of only three women to ever win both singles and doubles tennis in a single Olympic Games.

Five months before her wedding, Williams had an aggregate winning percentage of 85.76 percent. She had racked up seventy-two tournament wins on the Women's Tennis Association tour, including twenty-three Grand-Slam victories in twenty-nine singles finals and fourteen doubles finals with her sister Venus. Serena was considered by some sports experts to be the best tennis player in history. She had been ranked number one in the world longer than anyone other than tennis legends Steffi Graf and Martina Navratilova.

Alexis Ohanian was no slouch either. In 2005, at age twenty-two, he cofounded the social news website and discussion portal Reddit—a site dozens of media outlets and many in the tech world have called "the front page of the internet." A mere twelve years later, Reddit had mushroomed into the fifth-most-popular online destination, according to web analytic company Alexa, with more than 138,000 communities and more than 330 million active monthly visitors.

In the ten years after founding Reddit, Ohanian had his hands in a number of other groundbreaking ventures, too. In 2010, he helped launch the hit travel search website, Hipmunk. In 2011, he cofounded the early stage venture capital firm Initialized Capital. Just two years later, he became the bestselling author of *Without Their Permission: How the 21st Century Will Be Made, Not Managed*, a semiautobiographical book that explained how to harness the power of the webiverse for good. In some circles, the six-foot-five-inch (two-meter) tech guru was fondly referred to as the "mayor of the internet," according to Andy Greenberg of *Forbes*.

But despite their flawless-couple appearance, the road to their nuptials and beyond was far from easy. Both Williams and Ohanian endured devastating losses in their personal lives, which nearly derailed their careers. What's more, Williams suffered from a life-threatening illness that more than once almost killed her. Further, if they didn't just happen to be staying at the same hotel in Rome in 2015—she, to play at the Italian Open, and he, to attend a tech conference—the two never would have met in the first place.

INTRODUCTION

In one sense, Serena Williams and Alexis Ohanian come from two alternate universes. She's black; he's white. She plays sports; he's in tech. Yet despite their obvious differences in background and interests, their relationship works. It's a testament to the power of their love and their determination to join forces to take on the world and realize greatness.

Since the couple's fated union, millions of fans worldwide have taken notice, showering them with praise in person and on social media. Reporters have chimed in with their support, too. In April 2018, Candice Jalili of Elite Daily wrote, "Yeah, it's safe to say Ohanian loves Williams a lot. Here's to hoping we all find someone who loves, supports, and respects us the way these two do each other." E!News called Williams and Ohanian's romance "Absolutely swoon-worthy." But perhaps *InStyle*'s Sam Reed put America's collective admiration for the couple best. "With all due respect, no celebrity couple should be given the title [of power couple] unless their names are Serena Williams and Alexis Ohanian, he wrote in November 2018. "If you're looking for fairytale-like stories of romance, look no further than these two."

CHAPTER 1

MADE FOR THE COURT

Some little girls love to play dress up and put on makeup. Others are obsessed with reading books or have a soft spot for climbing trees and mucking around in the dirt. But Serena? She was made for the court.

Serena Jameka Williams was born on September 26, 1981, in Saginaw, Michigan, to Richard and Oracene Williams. She was the youngest of five daughters—an older sister, Venus, and three half sisters, Yetunde, Lyndrea, and Isha Price. The girls also had six stepsiblings from Richard's previous

MADE FOR THE COURT

As young girls, Williams sisters Venus (*left*) and Serena (*right*) learned to play tennis from their father, Richard. He taught them drills on courts near their home in Compton, California.

marriage, including older stepbrother Chavoita LeSane, who did not live with them.

Before Serena turned three, she and her family moved to a small house in Compton, a city in southern Los Angeles County, California. The sisters all shared one room and slept in two bunk beds, with Serena rotating between beds. Compton was known for its gangs and crime-ridden streets, but Richard used the area's grit to his advantage. He wanted to raise his girls to be mentally strong and "human tough" by teaching them how to stand up for themselves in any situation, he later told the *New Yorker*. "In the ghetto, no matter what color you are, you're gonna run for your life."

As soon as Serena and Venus could walk, Richard and Oracene taught the girls to play tennis—Serena at the age of three, Venus at the age of four. Richard had no professional training—he had taken rudimentary lessons before his daughters were born. But he read books and watched instructional videos to beef up his skills. He told the *New Yorker* that he put up motivational signs in the family's front yard ("Venus, You Must Take Control of Your Future" and "Serena, You Must Learn to Use More Top Spin on the Ball"). He also ripped off the heads of the girls' dolls to discourage any maternal fantasies. When Serena and Venus got older, they excelled in school but were not allowed to date. Instead, they accompanied the rest of the family to Kingdom Hall, the church of Jehovah's Witnesses, three times a week.

Despite this seemingly strict childhood, Serena flourished—especially at tennis. Every day, she and her family practiced drills together on the beat-up Compton courts, sometimes both before and after school. By 1991, Serena was 46–3 on the junior United States Tennis Association tour. She ranked first in the ten-and-under division.

For most people at that time, seeing an African American girl so young, let alone two, excel at tennis was almost unheard of. "There weren't a whole lot of African American tennis players on the circuit at

The Williams family, including Oracene (*right*), often played tennis together before and after Venus and Serena got home from school.

any age," Serena wrote in her autobiography, *On the Line*. "That goes back to the entitlement or privilege that attached to the sport." But for Serena, it wasn't a question of why she played, but how she could continue to get better, and better, and better. "I just remember playing, all the time," she wrote in *On the Line*. "It's like tennis was always there, like going to services at Kingdom Hall. Like breathing."

THE SERENA SLAM

Just before Serena turned ten, Richard and Oracene picked up the family and moved them to Florida so Serena and Venus could improve their game—first to Haines City, then to Pompano Beach. They hired Rick Macci, a professional tennis coach who was later inducted into the United States Professional Tennis Association (USPTA) Hall of Fame. Although Serena and Venus attended public school for the first few years of middle school, by the time Serena was in seventh grade, she and Venus were homeschooled by their mother. In between history lessons and English papers, they practiced their backhands and played against each other for hours every day on the courts near their home.

When Serena turned fourteen in 1995, Rick Macci and Serena's parents decided it was time she turned professional. She played a small tournament in Quebec City against Anne Miller in October and lost 6–1, 6–1. Serena wanted to keep up with Venus,

After the Williams family moved to Florida, Serena trained for hours every day with tennis coach Rick Macci.

SERENA WILLIAMS AND ALEXIS OHANIAN

who had made her professional debut a year earlier, but she wasn't ready. Still, there was an important lesson in the loss. "I could no longer expect to win. I'd have to earn it, fight for it. And I'd have to do it by myself," she wrote in *On the Line*. "No, when you're out there on the court in a tournament setting, for real, it's all on you."

With that determination, Serena set her mind to improving her game—and winning. In 1996, the Women's Tennis Association (WTA) ranked her number 304 in the world. A year later, at sixteen, she was ranked number ninety-nine. In 1998, she graduated high school and played her first Grand Slam tournament at the Australian Open. Although she lost to Venus in both rounds—6-7, 1-6—Serena wasn't ready to give up. By the end of the year, she was number twenty in the world. The following year, when she turned eighteen, she won her first Grand Slam in the US Open and had reached number four. According to *Teen Vogue*, she became the second African American woman to win a Grand Slam; the first was Althea Gibson in 1956.

> "I could no longer expect to win. I'd have to earn it, fight for it. And I'd have to do it by myself ... No, when you're out there on the court in a tournament setting, for real, it's all on you."
>
> —SERENA WILLIAMS

Despite her myopic approach to tennis and meteoric ascent up the ranks, Williams also took time to pursue other interests when she could. In 1998, she

MADE FOR THE COURT

In 2002, Serena (*right*) beat Venus in the Women's Singles Finals at Wimbledon. That same year, Serena also won the French Open and the US Open.

inked a $12 million contract with Puma to promote the company's shoes and tennis attire. A year later, at the behest of Venus, she enrolled at the Art Institute of Fort Lauderdale in Florida to pursue a degree in fashion design when time permitted. Though her intent was never to actually quit tennis in favor of fashion, the move would prove to be fortuitous—and a lifesaver—in the years to come.

Finally, in 2002, Williams reached a pinnacle in her career. The WTA ranked her the number-one female tennis player in the world. That same year, she

17

won the French Open, the US Open, and Wimbledon, and in 2003 she won the Australian Open, beating her sister Venus in the finals of each tournament. Media outlets around the world nicknamed the astonishing achievement the Serena Slam—the act of winning four Grand Slams in a row. She was one of only six women in the Open era, from 1968 to the present, to do so. Only three in the entire history of tennis actually accomplished the feat in the same calendar year: American Maureen Connolly Brinker in 1953, Australian Margaret Court in 1970, and German Steffi Graf in 1988.

TRAGEDY AND BURNOUT

Williams had moved mountains to become the best female tennis player on the planet. But by 2003, the emotional and physical stress of success was starting to wear on her. Her parents had divorced in 2002. The years of pounding across the court and whacking balls to her opponents at speeds upward of 120 miles per hour (193 kilometers per hour) had also taken its toll on her body. In the eight years since turning pro, Williams had sustained many injuries. In August 2003, ongoing pain in her knee and a dance mishap forced her to have reconstructive surgery.

Then a month later, tragedy struck. On September 14, Williams's half sister, thirty-one-year-old Yetunde Price, was murdered in a drive-by gang-related shooting in Los Angeles. Price was in the passenger seat of her boyfriend's SUV when a rash of gunfire broke out. One of the bullets struck her in the back of the head, killing her instantly. She'd been shot about 1.5 miles (2.4 km) from the tennis courts where her younger sisters learned to play the sport that made them world famous.

Williams and her family were devastated by the news. According to her autobiography, she slowly lost her motivation to play tennis. "Tennis was about the last thing on my mind, just then," she wrote in *On the Line*. "Forget that I wasn't physically ready to pick up a [racket]. It just didn't seem all that important." In between recovering from her knee surgery and dealing with a relationship breakup, Williams only played the occasional tournament. Because of her roller-coaster record, she dropped out of the top-ten rankings. Instead, she hung out at Stan's Donuts near her house, went to therapy, and dove deep into the New World Translation of the Holy Scriptures. According to an article in the *Guardian*, her only off-court "aerobic activity was shopping in Rodeo Drive." By 2006, with a world ranking of 139, she was prepared to call it quits.

But two major events saved Williams from succumbing to her depression. In 2004, she started working on her first clothing line, Aneres—"Serena" spelled backward. The Aneres launch on the Home Shopping Network didn't actually happen until 2009. But much of the design inspirations for the reasonably priced and fashion-forward dresses, tops, bags, and jewelry were sketched out during this time.

On December 15, 2004, Williams presented her Aneres Collection clothing line at The Forge, a world-famous restaurant in Miami Beach, Florida.

In 2006, Williams took a roots trip with Isha, Lyn, and their mother to Ghana and Senegal, on the coast of West Africa. With help from Oracene, Williams organized tennis clinics for kids in schools throughout the region. Working in tandem with UNICEF, she gave out polio vaccines, malaria pills, and vitamin A supplements at area hospitals. In Senegal, she also met with President Abdoulaye Wade and agreed to help him build a school that Senegalese kids could attend for free.

Williams wrote in her autobiography that she went on the trip because she hoped it would bring context and meaning to her life—and, in fact, the move worked. "Somehow, that first trip to Africa lifted me from my doldrums and set me back down on a positive path," she wrote. "I've been focused, determined, and boundlessly aware of how strong I am and how far I can go."

POSSIBLE RETIREMENT

Following her trip to West Africa and over the course of the next nine years, Williams rallied and triumphed. Her reputation as one of the world's best tennis players reached incredible heights. But her trajectory to stardom was not without its setbacks and disappointments, some of which nearly halted her momentum and ended her career.

In September 2009, Williams played a grueling match against Kim Clijsters in the US Open semifinals.

THE YETUNDE PRICE RESOURCE CENTER

When Yetunde Price was killed in 2003 by a senseless act of gun violence, she left behind three children and a vast community of relatives, friends, and neighbors who loved her. Thanks, in part, to her sisters' success and wealth, Yetunde's children had access to financial support to finish school.

But most other kids whose parents are killed by gangs or other types of abuse do not. So in 2016, as part of Williams Sisters Fund project, Serena and Venus created the Yetunde Price Resource Center both to honor their sister and to provide resources for Southern Los Angeles residents whose lives are directly or indirectly impacted by violence. The center connects people to free or discounted mental or physical healthcare services in the surrounding community. It partners with local schools and law enforcement officials to deliver community programs in violence prevention and conflict resolution. It also gives victims and at-risk individuals access to art therapy programs in poetry, creative writing, music and dance therapy, and theater.

During the second set, at 15–30, 5–6, a lineswoman called a foot fault on her second serve. Because of the call, two match points went to Clijsters. Williams was furious and began yelling profanities at the judge.

She had already received a conduct warning for throwing her racket during the first set. This time, she was docked a full point, costing her the game. To add insult to injury, the US Tennis Association fined Williams $10,000. Two months later, she was placed on a two-year probation and ordered to pay another $82,500 to the Grand Slam committee—the largest fine ever against a tennis player.

Then in 2010 and 2011, Williams was nearly taken down by myriad life-threatening health problems. Doctors found a blood clot in one of her lungs. She had multiple surgeries, including one to remove a hematoma (a massive swelling of clotted blood) and another to remove a lacerated tendon on her right foot. Though she used her time in recovery to publish a second memoir entitled *Queen of the Court*, she was in a lot of pain and off the courts for nine months.

Many in the tennis world thought Williams would retire. But once again, the tennis icon proved her fans and critics wrong. In July 2012, she won her fifth Wimbledon singles title and first major championship in two years. She played in the 2012 Olympics in London and earned her first gold medal, beating out Maria Sharapova in women's singles. By the end of 2012, she had captured fifteen Grand Slam singles titles and thirteen Grand Slam doubles titles. In June 2013, Williams took her second French Open title, as well as her sixteenth Grand Slam singles title. She won her third straight and sixth overall US Open singles title in 2014.

SERENA WILLIAMS: UNICEF AMBASSADOR

Ever since her first trip to West Africa in 2006, Serena Williams had been looking for more ways to give back to less fortunate people in communities around the world. On September 20, 2011, the twenty-nine-year-old was appointed a UNICEF International Goodwill Ambassador. As part of her duties, she helped build schools throughout Africa as part of the Schools for Africa program, as well as doing similar work for the Schools for Asia initiative.

"I believe all children deserve the chance to make something of their lives," Williams said in a statement. UNICEF executive director Anthony Lake couldn't have agreed with her more as he welcomed Williams to the stage at the Second Annual Social Good Summit in New York City. "Serena Williams isn't just a world tennis champion, she is a champion for children—and a passionate advocate for providing every child with a quality education," he said. "We are delighted that Serena is joining us as UNICEF's newest Goodwill Ambassador and look forward to working together to win for children."

By 2015, Williams was clearly on a roll. But something was about to happen that would alter the course of her life—and it wasn't about her career. It was a chance encounter that would not only change the way she thought about herself, but also shape her life forever.

CHAPTER 2

INTERNET WHIZ KID

Many sports experts have joked in their coverage of Serena Williams that the tennis icon must have been born with a racket in her hand. But the other half of America's beloved power couple—Alexis Ohanian—couldn't have been more dissimilar. Not one for sports aside from football, he was instead gifted at a young age with a mind for number crunching and puzzles. A superstar of a different sort, he staked his claim on history by cocreating a social aggregate news website called Reddit and revolutionizing the way people used the internet.

> As a child growing up in Ellicott City, Maryland, Alexis Ohanian earned a reputation at school and in his community for being an internet whiz kid.

Alexis was born on April 24, 1983, in the Fort Greene neighborhood of Brooklyn, New York. His mother, Anke, was born in Hamburg, Germany, and immigrated to the United States in 1976. His father, Christopher, was an Armenian American whose grandparents came to the United States as refugees after the Armenian genocide. Alexis was the couple's only child.

In 1986, before Alexis could barely read or write, his family moved to Ellicott City, a quaint planned community near Columbia, Maryland. Although he later played defensive tackle for Howard High School, Alexis spent most of his adolescence dreaming about playing the video game *Quake II* at all hours of the day. He finally convinced his parents to buy him a PC computer toward the end of middle school, claiming

INTERNET WHIZ KID

he needed one for his homework. From that point onward, he taught himself how to write code, learned HTML, and even started a small business creating websites for nonprofit organizations for free.

"No one knew I was this dorky kid in my parents' house in Columbia; they just knew I was someone who had a skill they didn't have," Ohanian explained at a talk he later gave at John Hopkins University in 2018. "I was doing it for fun, but also mostly for pride. My parents didn't have a totally clear idea of what I was doing, but they trusted me, which is really important, and they gave me agency to do this. It unlocked something very entrepreneurial in me."

During high school, Alexis did well in his studies—especially math and science. He got a part-time job at CompUSA, demonstrating software. "It was the worst public speaking experience a teenager going through puberty could have," he told the *New York Times*. "Every 30 minutes I'd have to get on a mic and demo to the whole store some lame piece of hardware or software and literally get ignored by people." From there he worked first as a dishwasher and cook at Pizza Hut, then got promoted to a waiter position. According to that same interview in the *New York Times*, Alexis's stint at the fast-food pizza restaurant taught him everything

> No one knew I was this dorky kid in my parents' house in Columbia; they just knew I was someone who had a skill they didn't have."
> —ALEXIS OHANIAN

SERENA WILLIAMS AND ALEXIS OHANIAN

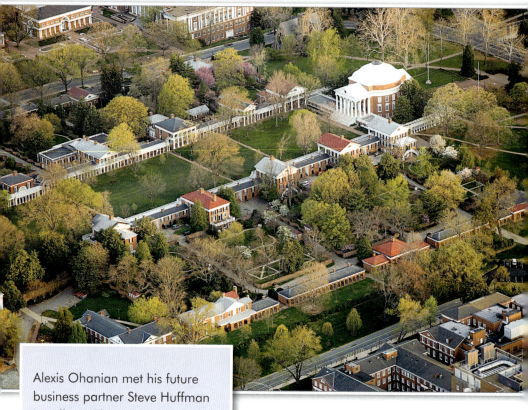

Alexis Ohanian met his future business partner Steve Huffman in college. The young men were roommates at the University of Virginia in Charlottesville, Virginia. The school's campus is pictured here.

he needed to know about customer service.

By the time Ohanian got to college at University of Virginia (UVA), he had switched gears—but only slightly. Though he still loved writing code and playing *Gran Turismo 2* in his spare time, he double-majored in history and German. His ultimate goal at the time was to go to law school and become an immigration lawyer.

Then fate stepped in. During his junior year in 2004, Ohanian was preparing to apply to law school and signed up for an LSAT prep course. He was taking a practice exam and got halfway through it before suddenly realizing he hated what he was learning. Without finishing the test, he got up, left, and went directly to Waffle House to clear his head. "It's a great place for epiphanies—and waffles," he told host Guy Raz on NPR's podcast *How I Built This*. "I had both there that morning, and realized if I wanted [those] waffles more than the LSAT, I probably shouldn't be a lawyer."

Ohanian's parents weren't pleased about their son's change of heart. But he didn't care. That decision to abandon law school in favor of following his dream to start a business permanently altered the trajectory of Ohanian's life.

A GENIUS IDEA

Over the course of his junior and senior years at UVA, Ohanian brainstormed business ideas with his roommate, Steve Huffman. Now with his law school aspirations firmly behind him, Ohanian was sure he and his friend could drum up something good. They started attending lectures and reading blogs by tech gurus on how to create a viable start-up. They also filled out an application to pitch some business ideas to Paul Graham, an entrepreneur from Boston, Massachusetts, who started tech incubator Y Combinator. Miraculously, they were called to Cambridge for an interview.

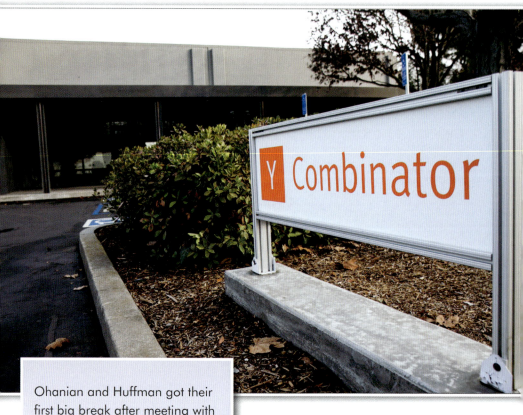

Ohanian and Huffman got their first big break after meeting with Paul Graham, founder of the tech incubator Y Combinator. An idea they pitched to Graham was the foundation of what eventually became Reddit.

The first idea Ohanian and Huffman pitched to Graham was a phone-based food-ordering system called My Mobile Menu. It might have worked as a mobile app. But because the iPhone hadn't yet been invented—it was 2005 and the first iPhone was released in 2007—the idea was rejected. Deflated and dejected, the two UVA seniors made their way back to Charlottesville, Virginia.

Again—fate came knocking. Halfway through their eighteen-hour train ride home, Ohanian and

Y COMBINATOR AND TECH FUNDING

A lot of people have ideas for how to start a company. But how many of them have enough guidance to carry the project through to completion? Even more important, how many projects have enough financial backing to actually succeed?

That's where Y Combinator comes in—and other companies like it. Every year, a large number of people apply for a spot in Y Combinator's tech start-up incubator program. Twice a year, the company invests $150,000 total in the projects that make the cut. The start-ups move to Silicon Valley and work with Y Combinator advisers to get their pitch into shape. The program culminates in a Demo Day, when the start-ups present their companies to potential investors. Many start-ups have succeeded thanks to Y Combinator's help, including Airbnb, Dropbox, Instacart, and Reddit.

Huffman got a call from Graham, who wanted them to return. When they finally arrived back at his office in Boston, a new kernel of an idea emerged. It would be a recommendation engine, of sorts, where users could post links to articles or sites they found interesting and discover or share others. The community would then rate each link. The most popular links would rise to the top and could be organized all in one place. According to *Vanity Fair*, at this point during the interview Graham said, "Yes. You guys need to build a front page of the internet." He gave them a check for $12,000 and told them to get started.

The rest of Ohanian's senior year was a blur. He and a couple of friends took a trip to Cancun. But mostly he and Huffman worked on their business plan. They experimented with names for the start-up,

After Reddit launched in 2005 and ballooned into one of the most popular sites on the internet, cofounders Ohanian (*right*) and Huffman gave dozens of interviews about the origins of their company's success.

including RipeFresh, Poplex, and PopTzar, but none of those made the cut. Perkle.com and aeonpop.com didn't work either. Finally they settled on Reddit. Though neither Ohanian nor Huffman was overly thrilled with the site's spelling, the name stuck.

After graduation, Ohanian and Huffman spent three months in Boston, working toward the launch. They sat in front of their computers for upward of fifteen hours a day, with breaks only to eat, sleep, and play *World of Warcraft*. Huffman built Reddit.com's back end, while Ohanian fiddled with the site's mascot and logo and tweaked the design elements.

During that time, Graham sent Ohanian and Huffman check-in emails—some good, some bad. According to *Vanity Fair*, one in particular must've gotten under their skin. "I don't know why you haven't launched yet; either you can't do it or you are waiting for it to be perfect, and I don't know which is worse," the note read.

It was the push they needed. In the third week of June, Ohanian and Huffman launched their company. Reddit.com was finally live. The website had a blue toolbar at the top that read "Reddit" in white letters. There were four navigation links: Profile, Browse, Submit, and Help. Compared to 2018 standards, the design was incredibly simple. But within just a few years, Reddit.com would blossom into one of the most popular websites in the world, valued at $1.8 billion, as reported by Kurt Wagner of CNBC.

REDDIT'S EVOLUTION: THE GOOD, BAD, AND UGLY

Since its launch in 2005, Reddit.com has gone through a series of unintentional makeovers, reflecting the changing values of the times. Throughout its tenure, the site has been used mostly by self-professed geeky males who post links or messages, then vote them up or down to reveal the most popular or meme-worthy content. At first, users and nonusers alike viewed the site as a massive and wonderfully addictive waste of time.

But that has started to change. For one, over the last ten years, Reddit has slowly become more political. "Above the links to videogame in-jokes, cat photos and screenshots of stupid Facebook behavior, visitors now often find links calling on the collective to take action on political issues where Reddit sees Washington suits meddling with a digital world they can't control and don't understand," reporter Andy Greenburg wrote in *Forbes* in 2012.

Unfortunately, the site has also become a venue for hate speech and discriminatory comments from users. Ohanian insists any type of harassment is banned from the site. But he also aims to encourage freedom of speech and open dialogue. He hopes to fight ignorance with discussion and the spread of fact-based knowledge. "Part of this is having a place where things can be said that I find incredibly disagreeable and reprehensible, but are still conversations that are happening right now online or offline in this country and in this world," he told the *New York Times*.

UPROOTED BY TRAGEDY

Launching Reddit was one of Ohanian's greatest moments in life. But it also coincided with three of the worst. A month into cocreating Reddit in the summer of 2005, Ohanian got a phone call from the mother of his then girlfriend. She was in tears. Her daughter had jumped from a fifth-floor balcony in Germany and was in a coma. Although she survived, she would never be the same.

That same year, Ohanian's dog died. Ohanian also received a second ominous phone call—this time, from his father. Ohanian's mother had suffered a seizure and was in the hospital. In trying to determine the cause, the doctors discovered an inoperable brain tumor. She was diagnosed with terminal brain cancer and didn't have long to live.

Over the next sixteen months, Ohanian's mother grew sicker and sicker. During that time, Ohanian and Huffman made the decision to sell Reddit to Condé Nast in 2006 for an undisclosed sum between $10 million and $20 million. The company's twenty-three-year-old cofounders went from being recent college graduates to multimillionaires virtually overnight. The first thing Ohanian did was to purchase four front-row season tickets around the fifty-yard line at FedEx Field, home to his favorite NFL team, the Washington Redskins. He also called his mother.

Anke Ohanian died on March 15, 2008. But not before her son had the chance to tell her that his start-up company had worked—and to share some of his money. "To be able to call her the morning after the money was in the bank and tell her my work was not in vain—and, moreover, that her support was not in vain—meant the world to me," he told *Inc*.

Ohanian stayed at Reddit after Condé Nast acquired it. But after three years, he decided he had had enough

> In 2010, Ohanian took a break from Reddit and spent four months in Armenia exploring his ancestral background. He returned to the country in 2015 to meet with students and talk about his work.

and needed a break from the tech world altogether. In 2010, Ohanian left Reddit and traveled to Armenia to explore his roots. He also spent four months there on a Kiva Fellowship, volunteering as a go-between for borrowers and lenders and getting hands-on experience in microfinance and social enterprise.

"Like many of the dogged Armenian activists, startup founders, journalists, and nonprofit workers I've met here, I don't want to dwell on Armenia's past—I want to help shape its future," Ohanian wrote in a blog post on Kiva's website during his time there. "I see microfinance as a way to export the best of capitalism to give many of the world's poor a chance to create their own futures."

"MAYOR OF THE INTERNET"

His time in Armenia brought Ohanian and his father closer and helped him get more of a sense of his family's ancestral history. It also taught him a wealth of much-needed skills to not only help grow his own business interests but others' as well. When Ohanian returned to the United States at the end of 2010, he launched or funded a number of projects that each in their own way sent shockwaves through the webiverse.

One of Ohanian's first endeavors was continuing to build and grow the audience for Breadpig, a

Kickstarter-like website that used crowdsourced money to fund various projects around the world. In a promotional YouTube video, the company described its mission as: "To help make the world suck less by selling you the geeky things you love and giving all the profits to good causes." That same year, he took on the travel industry with Reddit cofounder Steve Huffman and their mutual friend, M.I.T. graduate Adam Goldstein. After once again getting accepted to the Y Combinator program, the trio launched Hipmunk, a travel-booking website that claims it takes the headache out of searching for cheap fares on flights and hotel stays.

By 2011, Ohanian had put the tech world on notice. *Forbes* magazine named him in their annual "30 Under 30" list of movers and shakers in the industry, calling him the "mayor of the internet." Along with Garry Tan, Ohanian cocreated and launched the early stage venture capital firm Initialized Capital, which aimed to advise and fund other tech start-ups. Two years later, Ohanian published *Without Their Permission: How the 21st Century Will Be Made, Not Managed* and traveled to more than eighty universities over the course of five months to promote the book. The tour dovetailed nicely with his work as an angel investor—an adviser to fledgling entrepreneurs who need guidance or cash to launch their tech-related passion projects.

Despite having his hands in a number of projects, including briefly rejoining Reddit as executive chairman in 2014, Ohanian was also traveling constantly. As one of the most sought out speakers in the technology industry, he picked up speaking engagements at colleges, corporations, and conferences all over the world. In fact, it was during one of these business trips that fate would step in a third time—this time, for something good.

CHAPTER 3

A CHANCE ENCOUNTER

It was the morning of May 12, 2015. Thirty-three-year-old Serena Williams was staying at the lavish Cavalieri Hotel in Rome, Italy. That night, she was scheduled to play her first match in the Italian Open—and she was beyond annoyed.

The Cavalieri's delicious-looking breakfast buffet had closed just five minutes before Williams and her entourage—friend Jessica Steindorff, agent Jill Smoller, and business-development assistant Zane Haupt—arrived in the dining area. They had to sit in the pool area and order off the more limited menu

A CHANCE ENCOUNTER

instead. Then a tall, scruffy-looking man sat down at the table right next to them—the one they were saving for more members of their party who had yet to arrive. According to Williams, there were plenty of other empty spots in which to sit.

Rome, Italy, is one of the most majestic cities in Europe. For Williams and Ohanian, it's also the most romantic. They met in Rome on May 12, 2015.

That man was Alexis Ohanian. Unbeknownst to Williams, the tall intruder was a little hungover. He had stayed up until two in the morning drinking with actress Kristen Wiig, who was in Rome filming *Zoolander 2*. That morning, he had also missed the buffet breakfast and was planning on picking up a coffee, putting on his headphones, and working on his laptop to prepare for the speech he was giving at the Festival of Media Global conference later that day. Little did he know he had irritated the group next to him.

To try to get him to move, Haupt told Ohanian there was a rat under his table. (There wasn't.) The tactic didn't work—Ohanian lived in Brooklyn at the time and told them he wasn't afraid of rodents. In response, Williams laughed and addressed him directly: "No, we just don't want you sitting there. We're going to use that table," she said, according to *Vanity Fair*. Those were the first words she ever spoke to him.

Seeing the shocked look on his face, Williams backpedaled and invited him to come sit with them. The two talked about what she thought of Reddit (she sidestepped the truth that she had never been on the site) and what he thought of tennis (he danced around the fact that he had never watched a match on television or in real life). Eventually she gave him her number just in case she had any tech-related questions on revamping her newish website.

At the time, Williams was single, but had been seen flirting with music superstar Drake. She also assumed by the way he was acting that Ohanian was interested in Steindorff. He wasn't. According to *Vanity Fair*, Ohanian thought Williams was a

On the same day that Williams met Ohanian, she also won her match against Russian tennis player Anastasia Pavlyuchenkova—6–1, 6–3—at the Italian Open.

charming and beautiful woman. Still, he had just gotten out of a five-year relationship with his college sweetheart, microbiologist Sabriya Stukes, and he wasn't looking to start something new. He did go to Williams's match later that night. But both parties were positive that would be the end of their chance encounter—until it wasn't.

"DO I HAVE ANOTHER STALKER?"

Serena Williams and Alexis Ohanian were meant to be together from the beginning. But they also had a little help. After their breakfast encounter on May 12, agent Jill Smoller found out Ohanian was a client of William Morris Endeavor Entertainment, where she worked. So she invited him to Williams's tennis match—but she didn't tell Williams.

Following the game, Williams got into the van to head back to the hotel and was surprised to see Ohanian. At first, she suspected he was a stalker and freaked out. Then she thought he was a security guard. Finally, she recognized his scruffy face and realized he was the cute man from breakfast earlier that morning. Embarrassed, she invited him to dinner, but their schedules didn't match up—at least not yet.

FIRST DATE WHIRLWIND

Just a few days into the Italian Open, Williams ended up withdrawing from the tournament in the third round. Something was wrong with her right elbow, and she didn't want to risk further injury. Plus, the French Open was coming up in ten days and she needed to prepare.

"You know I hate, hate quitting, and this isn't quitting, it's just making a good decision," she told the Associated Press. "I was really injured last year, actually, and ended up taking like five days off before Paris and practicing just a day or two before the tournament started. And entering a Grand Slam, you never want to enter it like that, especially as defending champion."

There was something else Williams also needed to prepare for in Paris—a reunion with Ohanian. After she saw the lanky tech nerd in Rome, she couldn't get him off her mind. So she sent him a quick text, asking him to fly to Paris later that month to see her play.

Ohanian was positive something would get in the way of the rendezvous actually happening. Either that or Williams would end up blowing him off. "What's the worst that could happen? I know people in Paris, so if it doesn't work out, I'll have a great story to tell my friends about that time I almost hung out with Serena Williams," he told *Vogue*. But in the end, he went—and she didn't blow him off,

SERENA WILLIAMS AND ALEXIS OHANIAN

On one of the stops during their marathon first date, Williams and Ohanian strolled around La Ménagerie in the Jardin des Plantes, a zoo in Paris, France.

far from it. Instead, the two went on a whirlwind date full of delicious food, majestic sights, and plenty of flirting.

First they stopped at La Ménagerie in the Jardin des Plantes, a zoo in the middle of Paris, where Ohanian bought Williams some treats from a candy stall. Then they went to the iconic Eiffel Tower—a popular tourist attraction and one of the most romantic monuments in the world. Finally, they spent the next six hours just roaming the streets, popping into shops, munching on scrumptious snacks, and wandering wherever their hearts took them. It was a truly magical day and evening, both parties agreed. Without a doubt, they were mutually smitten.

THE FIRST DATE FROM OHANIAN'S PERSPECTIVE

In most articles about Williams and Ohanian's budding romance, the story is told from Williams's perspective. But on a May 8, 2018, taping of *The Late Show with Stephen Colbert*, the world finally got to hear it from Ohanian's side. Yes, he and Williams did visit a zoo. But he remembers the event as something a little more gruesome than she had ever let on in interviews.

> Ohanian told Colbert:
> There was this big cat, like a leopard, a majestic creature, and then it was feeding time. They threw out a bunny. It was a dead bunny, but it was a show. And this leopard just went in and blood is going everywhere. [Serena's] very romantic and she's standing in front of me and I can tell she's very unsettled by it. I said, "It's cool, we're going to keep going." But in that moment, I said, there's a connection. And in that moment, thanks to that poor rabbit, I found love, in spite of everything else.

SERENA WILLIAMS AND ALEXIS OHANIAN

THE ONE?

Williams won the 2015 French Open, beating out Lucie Safarova in the final. It was her twentieth Grand Slam title. But despite her clear exhilaration, she was also a little excited about something else—or someone.

After their magical day together, Williams couldn't stop thinking about Ohanian. "I had this sense, like, 'I'm going to marry this guy, but I'm not ready yet, but I know I'm going

In the beginning of their courtship, Ohanian tried to attend most of Williams's games in person, including this one at the US Open in Queens, New York, on September 11, 2015.

A CHANCE ENCOUNTER

to marry this guy,'" she told *InStyle*. She hoped the feeling was mutual—but she also didn't want to rush into anything too quickly and neither did he.

So they started texting and chatting every once in a while. Ohanian went to see Williams play in the US Open in September 2015. He shared a photo from the match on Twitter and Instagram, captioned "Come at the queen, you best not miss. #USOpen." Then he went to more of Williams's games. Before long, he barely missed watching a single one, whether live or on television. Still, though they tried to get together whenever their busy travel schedules permitted, the newish couple kept their dating status quiet on social media.

A BIRTHDAY TO REMEMBER

Alexis Ohanian turned thirty-two on April 24, 2015. He spent the evening with his grandparents, whom he adored. They went to the Carousel Restaurant in Little Armenia in Los Angeles for dinner.

But the evening was special for another reason. Williams called Ohanian using FaceTime to wish him a happy birthday.

> "I felt like a door had been opened to a person who made me want to be my best self ... I find myself just wanting to be better by simply being around her because of the standard she holds."
>
> —ALEXIS OHANIAN

(continued on the next page)

(continued from the previous page)

For most people, this isn't a strange occurrence. But Williams is a Jehovah's Witness—people who are Jehovah's Witnesses do not celebrate birthdays. Still, she called him anyway because it was important to him. He knew then that he wanted to marry her.

"I felt like a door had been opened to a person who made me want to be my best self ... I find myself just wanting to be better by simply being around her because of the standard she holds," he told *Vanity Fair*.

In late summer 2016, however, the world got their first clue that Williams and Ohanian were more than just chums. She posted a photo of him and all of her friends on Instagram in August. In November, she posted another photo of the two of them dressed up in bear-themed costumes for a Halloween party.

To anyone outside of the couple's family and close friends, it looked as though Williams and Ohanian were just beginning on the road toward true romance. But the reality was much different. In fact, Ohanian was planning an extra special surprise for Williams that not even she saw coming.

CHAPTER 4

THE YEAR OF CHANGE

At some point in every relationship, one person in the couple realizes it's time to get married. Sometimes it feels like a light bulb suddenly turning on. Other times, it's more like a firecracker exploding. But there's always a moment when one member first—or both members simultaneously—decide: This is it! We are gloriously happy! It's on! For Williams and Ohanian, it was definitely his move.

In early autumn 2016, Ohanian came up with what he thought was a foolproof surprise. He and Williams had been prone to taking impromptu

SERENA WILLIAMS AND ALEXIS OHANIAN

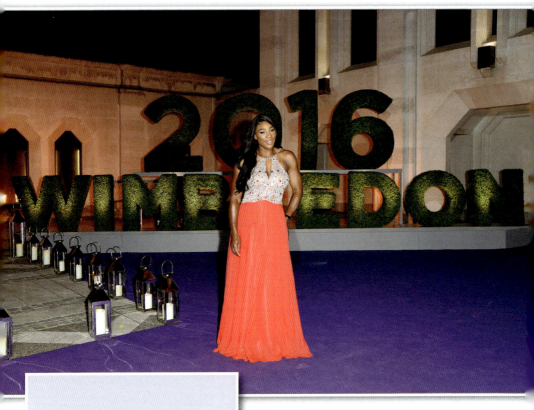

On July 10, 2016, Williams attended the Wimbledon Ball in London, England. Little did she know that four months later, Ohanian would pop the question.

vacations in the past, such as a recent trip to Disney World. Why not invite her to another whirlwind romantic evening, this time at the very place they met—the Hotel Cavalieri in Rome? When she least expected it, he would pop the question.

If all went according to plan, the idea could've worked. Williams was scheduled to play a match in India in December. So her friend Jill Smoller convinced Williams to stop over in Italy and meet Ohanian on the way back. But then the match was cancelled. Williams was exhausted. She was also busy preparing for the upcoming Australian Open in 2017 and begged Ohanian to scrap the trip.

Ohanian was having none of it. He insisted the plan was still a go. Furthermore, he had enlisted the help of Williams's friends, who knew about his intentions. Dakota Baynham, Williams's executive assistant, secretly threw a bunch of Serena's best clothes into some luggage. Tommy Hilfiger arranged a meeting with Williams at her house on the day she was supposed to leave, so he could gently but forcefully persuade her to get in the cab to the airport when it arrived. Jill Smoller was also in attendance for moral support (and more persuasive convincing).

According to *Vanity Fair*, Williams was annoyed by the disruption in her training schedule. In fact, her sour mood propelled her all the way to the airport. It wasn't until she was seated and the plane had taken off that the thirty-five-year-old realized what was probably coming. He was about to propose—and she was incredibly ecstatic about getting the chance to say yes.

When she arrived at the Cavalieri on December 10, Ohanian was there to greet her. He had reserved the same room they shared on a trip back a year earlier. Unbeknown to Williams, Ohanian had instructed the hotel staff to cover every surface in the suite with flowers. In true dramatic fashion, Ohanian led her to the pool area where they first met. On the same table where they once sat, he had propped a plastic rat. With a shaky voice, he retold the now-epic story of the moment they first laid eyes on each other. Then he got down on one knee and asked her if she would marry him.

She said yes.

"ISAIDYES"

When Serena Williams and Alexis Ohanian's friends and family heard the news that the adorable couple was getting hitched, they were over the moon with happiness. But Williams and Ohanian's fans and the rest of the world didn't find out about the exciting turn of events until a few weeks later, on December 29, when Williams revealed the news by posting a poem on Reddit.

The post was entitled "I said yes." At the top, there was an illustration of a nerdy cartoon character proposing to a cartoon tennis star, by handing her a giant diamond. Above the illustration were the words, "Future Mrs. Kn0thing." (Kn0thing is Ohanian's Reddit handle.) Below the illustration was a short-and-sweet rhyme about Ohanian's proposal and her acceptance.

The illustration received more than twenty-eight thousand points, propelling it to the front page of Reddit. The poem received nearly two thousand comments. The sweetest one of all was, of course, Ohanian's. "And you made me the happiest man on the planet," it said.

THE YEAR OF CHANGE

LIFE-CHANGING NEWS

It was the beginning of a new year, January 2017. After announcing their engagement, Williams and Ohanian were still wrapping their heads around the idea of "forever." Congratulations and well wishes from friends, family, and fans were still pouring in.

But Williams had other things to worry about as well. She was in Melbourne, Australia, preparing to play Venus in the Australian Open. She also needed to knock out the defending champion, Angelique Kerber. The only problem was she hadn't been feeling her usual self. Her joints ached. She felt nauseous. She figured it was the flu.

Her friend Jessica Steindorff, who was with her at the time, had other suspicions. She delicately

Talent manager Jessica Steindorff is one of Williams's closest friends. She is also the person Williams was with when the tennis star found out she was pregnant.

55

asked Williams if she suspected she might be pregnant. Williams thought Steindorff must have been joking. But two days later, after some subtle prodding and nudging, the tennis star finally agreed to take a pregnancy test to prove Steindorff wrong.

Williams was in her hotel room, getting ready for an event. The flashy affair was sponsored by the lingerie company Berlei, where Williams was the spokesperson for a line of sports bras. In between primping her hair and putting on eye makeup, she went to the bathroom and took the test. It came out positive, but she didn't trust the results. She continued getting ready. So Steindorff went to the hotel pharmacy and got another test. And another. And another. Finally, after the sixth positive result, the truth was crystal clear. Ohanian and Williams were about to become parents.

Williams called Ohanian immediately but didn't tell him the news. Instead, she suggested he come to Melbourne earlier than he originally planned. Thinking it was a health-related scare (but never expecting a pregnancy), he hopped on a plane right away to be at his soon-to-be wife's side. When he arrived, she handed him a small paper bag. Inside were the six pregnancy sticks, all showing plus signs.

Ohanian was overjoyed. Still, Williams had yet to compete at the Australian Open. A Grand Slam title and a world record were at stake. After checking with her doctor, who confirmed she was pregnant and estimated she was probably four weeks along—

THE YEAR OF CHANGE

On January 28, 2017, Serena Williams (*right*) beat her sister Venus in the Women's Singles Finals during the Australian Open. She did so while eight weeks pregnant. It was her twenty-third Grand Slam title.

she ended up being eight—Williams was given the green light to play. She didn't tell her coach, nor did she alert tournament officials. Instead, she played one of the toughest and most tiring series of games of her career. She won all seven matches, including the finals against Venus on January 28. It was her twenty-third Grand Slam title. She had finally beaten Steffi Graf's record for the most singles titles in the Open era.

"20 WEEKS"

> "You taught me the true meaning of serenity and peace. I can't wait to meet you ... From the world's oldest number one to the world's youngest number one.—Your Mommy."
>
> —SERENA WILLIAMS

On April 19, 2017, a photo posted on Snapchat shocked tennis fans around the world. The selfie showed Serena Williams posing in a mirror and wearing a bright yellow bathing suit. A baby bump was clearly visible. According to *People*, the caption underneath the photo read, "20 weeks."

Williams took the photo down immediately. She later explained to *USA Today* that the post was a mistake. She had been using the app to document how far along she was and had hit the wrong button. But it was too late—many of her followers had already seen the news. To make the pregnancy official, a spokesperson for Williams sent out a press release. "I'm happy to confirm Serena is expecting a baby this fall," the rep told *People*.

A week later, while on vacation in Mexico to celebrate Ohanian's thirty-fourth birthday, Williams posted a love note to their unborn baby on Instagram. "My Dearest Baby, You gave me the strength I didn't know I had," she wrote. "You taught me the true meaning of serenity and peace. I can't wait to meet you ... From the world's oldest number one to the world's youngest number one.—Your Mommy."

"She is so prolific on the court," Venus told *People* after her sister's win. "But now I am happy to watch her prepare for her wedding!"

A CLOSE CALL

In the months leading up to her delivery, Williams felt ecstatic about her future. She filled her soon-to-be baby's room with clothes, toys, and even their shared Australian Open trophy. But, as she explained to *Vogue* reporter Rob Haskell, she was also nervous about becoming a mother. Sure, she dreamed about having kids when she was a little girl. But what if the actual Momma Serena turned out to be too neurotic? How would she and Ohanian know what they were doing as first-time parents? What if the baby was unhealthy?

When the day finally arrived—September 1, 2017—Williams was nervous, but ready. But during the birth, a series of mishaps occurred. The baby's heart rate dropped dangerously low during contractions. Doctors performed an emergency C-section to prevent any further complications. The surgery went perfectly and Ohanian cut the umbilical cord. Baby Alexis "Olympia" Ohanian Jr. was born. "Before I knew it, Olympia was in my arms. It was the most amazing feeling I've ever experienced in my life," Williams later told CNN.

But the next day, as Williams was recovering after the birth, the trouble started. She felt short of breath

On May 1, 2017, Ohanian and a very pregnant Williams attended an art opening and gala at the Metropolitan Museum of Art in New York City.

and requested a CT scan. The test results revealed what she had most feared—a pulmonary embolism, a condition in which one or more arteries in the lungs becomes blocked by a blood clot. Then, due to bouts of intense coughing caused by the pulmonary embolism, Williams's C-section stitches popped open. When she returned to surgery to have the wound resealed, her doctors found a large hematoma within the tissues in her abdomen. In yet another return to surgery to fix that problem, doctors inserted a filter into one of her veins to prevent any more blood clots from traveling into her lungs and making the problem worse.

Williams survived the six-day ordeal. But when she finally landed back at home, she couldn't get out of bed for six weeks. Still, she was humbled. "I almost died after giving birth to my daughter, Olympia," she told CNN. "Yet I consider myself fortunate. I am so grateful I had access to such an incredible medical team of doctors and nurses at a hospital with state-of-the-art equipment. They knew exactly how to handle this complicated turn of events. If it weren't for their professional care, I wouldn't be here today."

As for Daddy Ohanian, he was also more relieved than he had ever been in his life. "I was happy to change diapers," *Vibe* reported. "But on top of everything [Serena] was going through, the feeling of not being able to help made it even harder. Consider for a moment that your body is one of the greatest things on this planet, and you're trapped in it."

A WORTHY CAUSE

According to UNICEF, 2.6 million newborns die each year around the world before their lives can even get started. More than 80 percent of those babies die from preventable reasons. According to the Centers for Disease Control and Prevention, African American women in the United States are more than three times more likely to die from pregnancy or childbirth-related causes. It is a problem—and a worthy cause—Serena Williams cares about deeply.

On February 20, 2018, CNN published a letter written by Williams. In it, she described the ordeal she endured while giving birth to Olympia. She also put out a call to CNN readers and implored them to educate themselves about the myriad problems facing women in the world today. As part of her role as a UNICEF goodwill ambassador, she asked people to donate to UNICEF and other organizations like it that were working toward solutions. "Every mother, everywhere, regardless of race or background deserves to have a healthy pregnancy and birth," she wrote. "Together, we can make this change. Together, we can be the change."

Olympia's birth was incredibly trying for both Williams and Ohanian. But now that their baby was in the world and healthy, the couple was ready to take on parenting. Would Williams

THE YEAR OF CHANGE

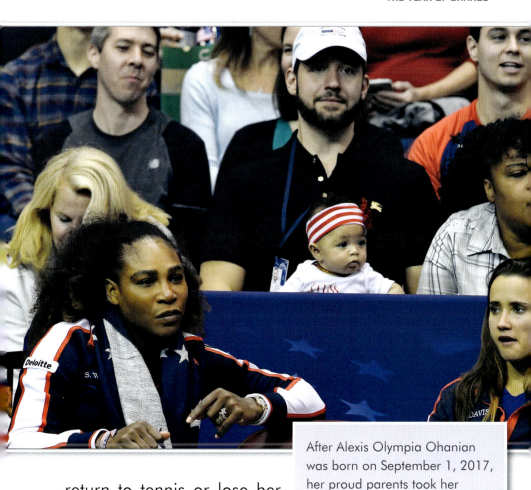

return to tennis or lose her momentum? Would Ohanian continue at Reddit or start yet another new venture? Only time would tell.

After Alexis Olympia Ohanian was born on September 1, 2017, her proud parents took her everywhere—including to watch a first-round Team USA vs. the Netherlands match in Asheville, North Carolina, during the 2018 Fed Cup.

The year to come would be challenging. Sometimes one or both of them would nearly reach their breaking point. But because of their individual strength and collective love for each other, they could weather the ups and downs together.

"I almost died. But now [Olympia's] the reason why all of this means even more than it did before," Williams said in the first episode of the HBO documentary *Being Serena*, entitled "Fear." "Still—there's no escaping the fear. The fear that I might not come back as strong as I was. The fear that I can't be both the best mother and the best tennis player in the world. I guess my only choice is to live and find out."

But first, the wedding!

CHAPTER 5

FULL-TIME PARENTS

It was 3:00 p.m. on November 15, 2017—the day before the big event. According to Alexandra Macon of *Vogue*, workers were bustling around the Contemporary Arts Center of New Orleans in Louisiana, fiddling with last-minute touches and making sure everything was perfect. Williams and Ohanian were inside practicing their first dance to "Tale as Old as Time" one last time. The paparazzi were buzzing around like busy bees outside the venue, readying their cameras in the hopes that they could get a stellar photograph or two of the famous power couple.

The next day, Williams and Ohanian would tie the knot, with eleven-week-old baby Olympia in tow. Not only would it be a day of celebration for their new family, but also a remembrance and tribute to Ohanian's mother, who had died nine years earlier. "[November 16] is her birthday, and we wanted her to be represented at the wedding," Williams told *Vogue*. "Obviously, we wish that she could be here for this, but choosing her birthday as our wedding date was a nice way of making sure she's still involved and made us feel more connected to her on our day."

At 5:15 p.m. on November 16, guests started arriving. Jay-Z, Beyoncé, and Beyoncé's mother, Tina Knowles; Kelly Rowland; Kim Kardashian West; Anna Wintour; Ciara; Eva Longoria; and La La Anthony were just some of the celebrities who were in attendance. The room was decorated in a *Beauty and the Beast* theme, with a fashion-show runway in the center and couches and comfortable chairs surrounding it on three sides. Before the ceremony began, a video explaining the story of Williams and Ohanian's courtship played on TVs encased in glitzy frames above the aisle.

After the video concluded, the bridesmaids made their entrances, wearing Galia Lahav dresses. Williams's best friend, Val Vogt, carried the bride's Yorkshire terrier, Chip, down the aisle in his own little tuxedo. Williams's mother carried little Olympia, who was decked out in a white dress with sparkly jewels around the waist and sleeves and matching booties.

Williams and Ohanian tied the knot at the Contemporary Arts Center, a historic building in the arts district of New Orleans, Louisiana.

Then, it was the moment everyone had been waiting for: Williams appeared in a pristine white, princess-style strapless Sarah Burton for Alexander McQueen dress, with a matching sheer cape. She carried a bouquet of white roses and slowly walked toward Ohanian, who looked dashing in his Giorgio Armani suit and dark blue velvet jacket. As the couple reunited under a canopy of yellow, orange, and white flowers, they recited their vows to each other with tears in their eyes.

Ohanian told his soon-to-be wife, according to *USA Today*:

> You are the greatest of all time, not just in sport. I'm talking about as a mother and as a wife. I am so excited to write so many more chapters of our fairy tale together. And my whole life I didn't even realize it, but I was waiting for this moment. And everything that I have done, everything that I am so proud of in my career, and in my life, for the last thirty-four years, pales in comparison to what we're doing today.

By the time they were finished, there wasn't a dry eye in the audience. When the couple was pronounced husband and wife, everyone cheered. The ceremony was perfect—but then it was time to party!

> "I am so excited to write so many more chapters of our fairy tale together. And my whole life I didn't even realize it, but I was waiting for this moment."
>
> —ALEXIS OHANIAN

PARTY TIME

After the ceremony, the guests piled into a separate ballroom area for dinner. There were four banquet tables named after Williams's Grand Slam wins, each of them covered with gorgeous centerpieces of yellow and purple flowers. Chandeliers encased in gold birdcages hung above

FASHION QUEEN

When most people think of tennis icons, they think of sneakers, shorts, and athletic gear—not fancy ball gowns. But due, in part, to Williams's background in fashion design, she wanted her wedding attire—and that of her wedding party—to be extra stylish. Williams's friends swore she was a laid back bride-to-be. Still, she worked with some of the fashion industry's top designers when planning her outfits.

After the ceremony, Williams changed into a dramatic and semifitted A-line dress designed by Versace for the reception. It was made by a team of five expert embroiderers and covered in delicate beads, with feathered accents. According to *Vogue*, it took a total of 1,500 hours to create.

Versace also designed Williams's third dress for the evening. It was white and short with a flouncy skirt for a flawless, swirly spin. Williams topped off the outfit with bejeweled Nike tennis shoes—perfect for dancing.

the tables, while trophy-style name cards lined each plate. The band played "Be Our Guest" as everyone found his or her seats. Ohanian and Williams sat in two gold throne-like chairs at the head of one of the tables.

After a buffet-style meal of Armenian, Southern, Italian, and other types of food, the newlyweds

Tony Award–winner Cynthia Erivo was just one of the distinguished guests who performed at Williams and Ohanian's star-studded wedding.

showed off their moves and pulled off their first dance perfectly. A performance by New Edition was a thrilling surprise, especially after Williams and Ohanian joined them on stage for a number. Tony Award–winner Cynthia Erivo also sang her rendition of "A Natural Woman."

BEING SERENA

In the months leading up to a wedding, many people are nervous for what's to come. So much planning. So many things to think about! But for Serena Williams, those moments were even more magnified because they were caught on tape.

In a five-part HBO documentary series entitled *Being Serena*, the camera gives viewers access into some of the sports star's most private moments. Intimate shots of her pregnancy, her wedding, even some close-ups during Olympia's birth are shown. What's more, Williams shares some of her deepest thoughts, including her fears about being a good mother and her frustration at not being able to play like she once did at the height of her career. While the documentary mainly focuses on Williams, Ohanian is given screen time, too. As she says in the first episode of *Being Serena*: "Everything starts with love. I feel like we have an unbelievable respect for each other and I think that's the basis of any relationship."

Toward the end of the evening the space transformed yet again into a lounge for the after-party. DJ Mike Wise played 1990s-era rap on the turntables, while actual pyramids of donuts dropped down from the ceiling in case guests got hungry. But the real showdown of the evening happened at 1:30 a.m.—a surprised cooked up by Ohanian for his new bride. Ohanian grabbed the mic to get everyone's attention. A curtain dropped. The lights went up to reveal a giant, all-white carousel, while Ginuwine's "Pony" played in the background.

Everyone gasped. Williams screamed with glee. It was truly a magical moment and the perfect cap to a fairytale evening that the newlyweds would never forget.

LEARNING TO BE PARENTS

In the weeks following the wedding, Williams and Ohanian were still coming down from all the excitement. But they were also getting used to the idea, and the reality, of having a baby in the house. Williams's mother moved in temporarily to help with the adjustment. Venus and the rest of Williams's sisters were close by as well, in case any additional help was needed. Still, learning how to change diapers, not to mention how to adapt to a hungry and crying newborn at all hours, proved difficult for the new parents at first.

Ohanian had to get used to his new role as a father. But the internet mogul quickly learned a few key tricks, including that hands-free baby carriers are key for multitasking.

According to the documentary *Being Serena*, Williams also felt frustrated by her ongoing health problems. Though she eventually recovered from the C-section and her strength slowly returned, she still felt sluggish and out of shape. She got tired much more quickly. Although she was mentally ready to get back to playing tennis, her body hadn't yet caught up. "For so many years I defined myself in just one way—my success, my championships, my making history. Then, all of a sudden, my life changed forever," she said in the first episode of *Being Serena*.

Ohanian, of course, had none of the bodily changes to contend with. But emotionally, it felt like a rollercoaster for him, too. After Olympia's birth, he went through a true transformation. He said in an interview at the Commonwealth Club:

> I did not realize just how much it would change my life. Very quickly I went from being, you know, very selfish and sort of about-me, to now having a wife and child … I really felt a new level of responsibility and it was exhilarating because it made the work and my career—which I'm so proud of and which I thought was the most important thing—it actually [made me realize] one, it wasn't the most important thing, but two, it gave it a purpose that was so much bigger than just me.

DEDICATED TO FATHERHOOD

In dozens of interviews and articles since his daughter was born on September 1, 2017, Alexis Ohanian has expressed an outpouring of love for his family and joy at becoming a father. But he has also been outspoken in his belief that the maternity and paternity laws in the United States are far from ideal. Though he took sixteen paid weeks off from work and Williams took seven months off from playing tennis full time, Ohanian is well aware that most people don't have that luxury.

The United States is the only industrialized nation that doesn't have a mandatory paid parental leave policy for new parents. According to the nonprofit group Paid Leave for the US, a quarter of new mothers go back to work within ten days of delivery. In an op-ed piece for *The Hill*, Ohanian wrote:

> Whether you're in the C-suite or just starting out in the workforce, you should be able to prioritize your family when they need you … This is more than just about doing the right thing—it's a smart business decision. We employ humans, not robots, and if you're expecting them to do great work, they need to be in a healthy state of mind."

But slowly, the couple adjusted—and they got better at being parents. They sang "Rubber Ducky" songs while bathing Olympia in the tub. They took her on long walks around the neighborhood and showed the baby off to family and friends. On most nights, Williams breastfed while Ohanian cooked his wife dinner.

Williams also got back on the court, first just running drills for a few hours in the morning with a trainer. She couldn't serve as hard as she used to. Her backhand wasn't as powerful. She desperately wanted to shed some of the baby weight she had gained. But day by day, her energy increased and her body felt stronger.

In late December 2017, the family took their first tennis-related trip. For the first time ever, a women's tennis match was being held in Abu Dhabi, the Mubadala World Tennis Championship. Williams knew she wasn't in good-enough shape to win. But she hoped her first match back in the professional realm would give her a sense of how far she needed to go to get back to where she needed to be. In addition, women's rights was an issue Williams deeply cared about. For her, it was an important event to attend—win or lose. "It was really strictly to send a message that women can be strong, you can do what you want, and you can dream big," she said in the third episode of *Being Serena*.

On December 30, 2017, in Abu Dhabi, Williams played her first professional match after becoming a mother. Although she lost, she was nonetheless determined to regain her status as the queen of tennis.

Williams lost the match to Jelena Ostapenko. But she wasn't giving up, not by a long shot. Neither was Ohanian. In the months to come, big changes would take place in Ohanian's work life. Throughout all of it he continued to grapple with important questions, such as how to juggle being a loving and hands-on father with moving forward professionally and embodying one of the most visible and influential businessmen in the world.

As for Williams, she had her eyes on a new prize, too. Of course, she would continue to spend every waking moment she could taking care of Olympia. But she was also more determined than ever to achieve an epic milestone. She was committed to winning twenty-five Grand Slams to beat Australian Margaret Court's world record.

Balancing parenthood with work would be hard for both Williams and Ohanian. But they'd get there in due time. The power couple would be able to accomplish the seemingly impossible because they had each other.

CHAPTER 6

A MATCH MADE FOR WINNING

In the year since Olympia was born, life was still in turmoil for Ohanian and Williams. In January 2018, Ohanian went back to work full time at Reddit, only to step down from his daily duties for good a month later. Although he kept his position on Reddit's board, he made the decision to leave the company to focus more on his work for Initialized Capital, the early-stage venture capital firm he cofounded in 2011.

"I had a pretty productive last year, personally, when it came to getting married, as well as having a baby," Ohanian told the *Wall Street Journal*. "I came back from parental leave at the start of January, and really started thinking about where I wanted to be, what I wanted to be doing."

While Ohanian is clearly 100 percent devoted to his family, his mind is also beginning to refocus on business. In the past six years, his entrepreneurial work has influenced significant change in the world—and has made many people's lives easier. Initialized Capital has funded and given guidance to more than two hundred start-ups, including same-day grocery delivery service Instacart, digital currency exchange Coinbase, and an app called Opendoor that is on its way to revolutionizing the real estate business.

In July, Ohanian announced an entrepreneur contest in partnership with upscale coffee brand Folgers 1850. The winning idea will get $18,500 in funding, as well as a one-on-one mentoring session with the thirty-five-year-old start-up guru. For a guy whose net worth is $9 million, as reported by MarketWatch, Ohanian insists he wants to use his financial wherewithal and skills to help make the world a better place. "It's a fine line, but these ideas do have to be bold: If you are hearing about these businesses for the first time, it's going to, in some way, change your view of the world, because it will challenge the belief of how things should be," he told MarketWatch.

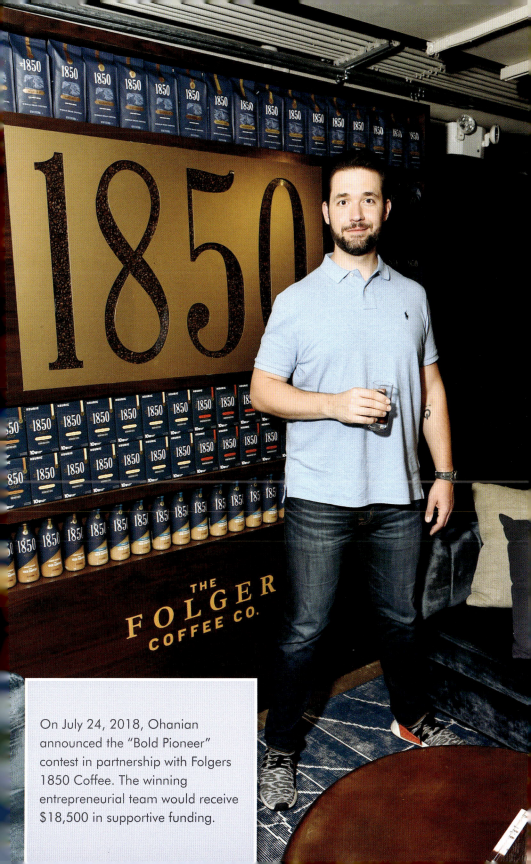

On July 24, 2018, Ohanian announced the "Bold Pioneer" contest in partnership with Folgers 1850 Coffee. The winning entrepreneurial team would receive $18,500 in supportive funding.

CLIMB TO THE TOP

While Ohanian has been busy commuting back and forth from his family's home in Florida to Initialized Capital's office in the Bay Area since going back to work full time, thirty-seven-year-old Williams has been trying to step back into her game. She missed the Australian Open in January 2018 because she wasn't physically up to it. But by February she was

In April 2018, Williams released a five-part documentary series about her life, love, family, and career called *Being Serena*. It aired on HBO and attracted millions of viewers worldwide.

gearing up for one of the biggest tournaments of the year outside of the Grand Slams—Indian Wells in California.

On February 27, as she was driving on California's I-10 freeway outside of Palm Springs, she looked up and saw a startling sight: a billboard-sized photo of her and Olympia. Then another. And another. The three billboards spelled out "Greatest Momma of All Time." On the fourth, there was another picture of Williams holding her baby, with the caption: "Serena Williams: G.M.O.A.T - Alexis Jr. + Sr." He also alerted the world with a post on Instagram and Twitter.

According to Williams, it was just the push she needed to feel more confident, be more confident—and it was also incredibly endearing. "Literally am crying," the tennis icon wrote in reply to Ohanian's post. "This is so sweet. I love you."

Williams didn't end up winning the Indian Wells tournament. She lost to Venus in round three. According to the fourth episode of *Being Serena*, Serena was devastated—and frustrated that she couldn't just pick up where she left off before having a baby. But as her coach, Patrick Mouratoglou, kept reminding her, if she wanted to make tennis a priority again, she would need to figure out a way to have her new family fit into her tennis schedule rather than the other way around.

RACISM ON THE COURTS

The Indian Wells tournament was significant to Williams for many reasons. It was her first major game back after becoming a mother. But it was also a chance for her to make peace with her past to create a more present and powerful future.

In 2001, Williams and Venus were scheduled to play against each other in a tournament at Indian Wells. But Venus withdrew because of an injury. At the time, there were rumors the girls' father was fixing his daughters' matches. Though the rumors weren't true, the crowd was still furious. They booed Serena every time she walked onto the court to play.

"Was there racism behind it? Yeah, absolutely," she said in the fourth episode of *Being Serena*. "We were always outsiders. I don't think anyone knew what to do with these two black sisters and their daddy—a strong, proud black man."

Williams swore she'd never return to Indian Wells. Yet she did. For her, after Olympia, it was time to forgive and start again.

But Williams, whose net worth clocks in around $150 million, according to MarketWatch, is slowly but surely finding a healthy balance. She's taking on other projects, too. Following her collaborations with the Home Shopping Network and helping to design her tennis uniforms for Nike, she launched a new clothing line in May 2018. Called Serena, her debut twelve-piece collection is sleek yet semiaffordable, with prices ranging from $35 for a shirt to $250 for a dress. Some of the items were inspired by the #MeToo movement and have motivational slogans on the sleeves or legs, such as "I am beautiful, I am strong."

"The customer is a girl or a woman who believes in herself, or wants to believe in herself," Williams told *WWD*. Because the line was designed by Williams, who has been a role model to so many girls and women around the world, the items are already selling out fast on the tennis star's website.

FASHION FAUX PAS?

Serena Williams is known for her stylish tennis outfits—especially the ones she designed in collaboration with Nike. But in the 2018 French Open the president of the French Tennis Federation, Bernard Giudicelli, criticized Williams for wearing a body-hugging *Black Panther*-inspired catsuit during a match. He even went a step further and banned catsuits from the tournament altogether. "One must respect the game and the place," he said, according to the Huffington Post.

People all over the world were outraged by the implied sexism in the decision, especially since Williams insisted she wore the catsuit to prevent

(continued on the next page)

SERENA WILLIAMS AND ALEXIS OHANIAN

(continued from the previous page)

During the 2018 French Open, officials banned body-hugging attire after Williams wore a *Black Panther*-inspired catsuit. Fans everywhere were outraged by the implied sexism in the decision.

blood clots from forming and endangering her health. (Although she did admit to the *Guardian* that wearing it did make her feel like a warrior princess.) Former tennis star Billie Jean King came to Williams's defense on Twitter, tweeting the "policing of women's bodies must end" and that "criticizing what she wears to work is where the true disrespect lies."

In the end, Williams is the one who had the last laugh. In the first round of the US Open on August 27, 2018, she strutted out onto the court in NikeCourt Flare trainers, fishnet compression tights, and a custom-designed tutu by Louis Vuitton designer Virgil Abloh and Nike. Her fans loved her for it.

A PATH FORWARD

On September 1, 2018, Olympia turned one. Ohanian was still commuting and working at Initialized Capital. He was still surprising his wife with unforgettable vacations to places like Venice, Italy. And he was still posting adorable photos on Instagram and writing gushing tweets to his wife and daughter on Twitter to make even the most coldhearted person swoon. For him, his family is where it's at, always and forever—and he couldn't be happier about it.

As for Williams, she's head-over-heals in love, too. Yes, her femininity is still called into question from time to time—*GQ* named her its 2018

SERENA WILLIAMS AND ALEXIS OHANIAN

> Ohanian is his wife and daughter's number-one fan.

"Woman" of the Year on the magazine's cover (the quotation marks caused an uproar with fans). She also has hit a few hiccups in her career—she lost the US Open in the finals to twenty-year-old Naomi Osaka because of a technicality in September 2018; got into a verbal argument with the chair umpire; and ended up getting fined $4,000 for supposedly receiving advice from her coach during the match, $3,000 for throwing her racket, and $10,000 for verbal abuse. Still, Williams is taking the setbacks in stride. No, she hasn't retaken the throne as the queen of tennis. But she's getting closer with every tournament and insists that the feat—and winning her twenty-fifth Grand Slam—is on the horizon.

It's tempting to ask what makes this power couple succeed. Is it the undying love and mutual respect

A MATCH MADE FOR WINNING

Williams and Ohanian clearly have for each other? Is it that they both try to be the best they can be in their careers and support each other along the way? Or is it a little bit of both? Maybe Williams's thoughts to her daughter at the end of *Being Serena* sums up the reason why the couple works together perfectly: "Whether I win or lose, you're with me out there … [Your] daddy and you, you're my people. You make me stronger. You make me tougher. You make me better. Now let's see what we got baby—together."

> **Whether I win or lose, you're with me out there … [Your] daddy and you, you're my people. You make me stronger. You make me tougher. You make me better. Now let's see what we got baby—together."**
>
> **—SERENA WILLIAMS**

TIMELINE

1981 Serena Williams is born on September 26.

1983 Alexis Ohanian is born on April 24 in Brooklyn, New York. His family moves to Maryland three years later.

1995 Williams plays her first professional tennis match at age fourteen.

1998 Williams graduates high school and plays her first Grand Slam tournament at the Australian Open.

1999 Williams wins the US Open on September 12, becoming the first Williams sister to win a Grand Slam.

2002 Twenty-year-old Williams is ranked the number-one female tennis player in the world for the first time. She also wins a Serena Slam—four Grand Slam tournaments in a row.

2003 Yetunde Price, Williams's older half sister, is killed in a drive-by shooting in Compton, California.

2004 Williams launches the Aneres clothing line. Ohanian has the Waffle House moment and realizes he doesn't want to go to law school.

2005 Ohanian and his college roommate Steve Huffman cofound Reddit. A few weeks later, he finds out his mother has terminal brain cancer.

TIMELINE

2006 — Williams takes a trip to West Africa with her mother and sisters, in tandem with UNICEF. Ohanian and Steve Huffman sell Reddit to Condé Nast for more than $10 million.

2008 — Ohanian's mother dies on March 15.

2009 — Williams publishes her autobiography *On the Line*. She also gets fined $10,000 by the US Tennis Association and $82,500 by the Grand Slam Committee, for her poor behavior in a US Open match.

2010 — Ohanian leaves the tech world and goes to Armenia as part of a Kiva Fellowship. When he returns, he helps launch travel search website Hipmunk.

2011 — Ohanian is listed in *Forbes* magazine's "30 Under 30" list. He and Garry Tan cofound Initialized Capital. Williams undergoes emergency surgery for a blood clot in her lungs. Later that September, she is appointed a UNICEF international goodwill ambassador.

2012 — Williams wins her first gold medal in the Olympics.

2013 — Ohanian publishes *Without Their Permission: How the 21st Century Will Be Made, Not Managed* and travels to more than eighty universities to promote it.

SERENA WILLIAMS AND ALEXIS OHANIAN

2014 Ohanian rejoins Reddit as executive chairman.

2015 Williams and Ohanian meet in a chance encounter at the Cavalieri Hotel in Rome, Italy, on May 12.

2016 Williams ties Steffi Graf for most singles titles in the Open era. Ohanian proposes to Williams on December 10 in Rome. On December 29, they announce their engagement to the world.

2017 In January, Williams beats Venus in the Australian Open final and collects a twenty-third Grand Slam title to surpass Graf for the Open Era lead. Alexis Olympia Ohanian Jr. is born on September 1. Williams almost dies in surgery, but recovers. Williams and Ohanian get married on November 16.

2018 Ohanian rejoins Reddit in January, quits again, but remains on the board. Instead, he focuses on his work at Initialized Capital. Williams begins playing tennis again full time. Williams is named by GQ as its 2018 Woman of the Year.

GLOSSARY

aggregate In sports, a score calculated by adding the results of several matches.

code Programming instructions for a computer.

C-section Short for caesarean section; a surgical procedure used when it would be too risky for the mother or baby to deliver vaginally.

epiphany A sudden realization or bright idea.

foot fault When a tennis player gets penalized for incorrect placement of the feet when he or she is serving the ball.

fortuitous Fortunate; happening by a lucky chance or for a good reason.

Grand Slam A set of major tennis championships or matches in the same year.

HTML Short for hypertext markup language; a computer language that allows computer programmers to set text color, font types, hyperlinks, graphics, etc.

impromptu Done without preparation or being planned; often a surprise gesture.

inducted Admitted into an organization or group.

lineswoman A female official who assists the umpire in tennis.

meme An often funny image, video, or piece of text that is copied and quickly circulated by internet users.

microfinance a type of banking service that is given to people or groups who are unemployed or have low incomes and would otherwise have no other access to money.

myopic Single-minded; incredibly focused.

myriad Many in number.

paparazzi Photographers who work for themselves and pursue celebrities to get photographs of them.

pinnacle Peak; the most successful point.

rendezvous A meeting, usually between two people, at an agreed upon time or place.

rudimentary Basic; elementary.

start-up A newly formed business.

tech incubator A company or group that helps other fledgling companies or people get their business started by lending money or advice.

venture capital Money invested in a project in which there is a high element of risk, typically a new or growing business.

webiverse A popular slang word for the internet.

FOR MORE INFORMATION

Girls Who Code
28 West 23rd Street, 4th Floor
New York, NY 10010
Website: https://girlswhocode.com
Facebook, Instagram, and Twitter:
   @GirlsWhoCode
Girls Who Code is an organization dedicated to closing the gender gap in technology and tech-related endeavors. In chapters across the United States and expanding into Canada, girls in middle school and high school learn computer-programming skills and gain access to science, technology, engineering, and mathematics (STEM) career guidance.

International Tennis Hall of Fame
194 Belleview Avenue
Newport, RI 02840
(401) 849–3990
Website: https://www.tennisfame.com
Facebook and Twitter: @TennisHallofFame
Instagram: @tennishallofame
YouTube: @tennisfamer
The International Tennis Hall of Fame is an interactive museum dedicated to promoting the history of tennis and celebrating its champions. Exhibits include images, videos, and more than two thousand trophies, uniforms, and other artifacts from the museum's collection.

Reddit
520 Third Street, Suite 305
San Francisco, CA 94107
Website: https://www.reddit.com
Facebook, Instagram, and Twitter: @reddit
Reddit is a social news aggregate and destination with thousands of communities in which users can discuss sports, breaking news, entertainment, and more.

United Nations International Children's Emergency Fund (UNICEF)
3 United Nations Plaza
New York, NY 10017
(212) 326-7000
Website: https://www.unicef.org
Facebook, Instagram, and Twitter: @UNICEF
UNICEF works in 190 countries and territories to help provide children with sufficient resources to survive, maintain their rights, and fulfill their potential, from early childhood through adolescence. Programs focus on education, social inclusion, gender equality, and poverty assistance.

Women's Sports Foundation
247 West 30th Street, 5th Floor
New York, NY 10001
(800) 227-3988
Website: https://www.womenssportsfoundation.org

FOR MORE INFORMATION

Facebook and Instagram:
WomensSportsFoundation
Twitter: @WomensSportsFdn
Founded in 1974 by tennis legend Billie Jean King, the Women's Sports Foundation is dedicated to creating leaders by ensuring all girls access to sports.

Women's Tennis Association (WTA)
100 Second Avenue South, Suite 1100-S
St. Petersburg, FL 33701
(727) 895-5000
Website: http://www.wtatennis.com
Facebook, Instagram, and Twitter: @WTA
The WTA is the global leader in women's professional tennis with more than 2,500 players representing nearly one hundred countries around the world. It was formed in 1973 by tennis legend Billie Jean King, who aimed to unite the sport in one tour.

Y Combinator
320 Pioneer Way
Mountain View, CA 94041
Email: info@ycombinator.com
Websites: https://www.ycombinator.com; https://www.start-upschool.org
Facebook and Twitter: @YCombinator
YouTube: Y Combinator
Y Combinator provides early-stage funding,

guidance, and advice for start-ups. The company also offers a free online start-up course called Start-up School.

Yetunde Price Resource Center
363 West Compton Boulevard
Compton, CA 90220
(310) 554-4638
Email: info@ypresourcecenter.org
Website: https://www.yprcla.org
The Yetunde Price Resource Center was founded by Serena and Venus Williams to honor their sister. It is a community center for residents in Southern Los Angeles County who have been affected by violence or trauma.

For Further Reading

Boehme, Gerry. *Serena Williams: Setting New Standards* (At the Top of Their Game). New York, NY: Cavendish Square, 2017.

Cline-Ransome, Lesa, and James Ransome. *Game Changers: The Story of Venus and Serena Williams*. New York, NY: Simon & Schuster Books for Young Readers, 2018.

Cunningham, Meghan Engsberg. *Serena Williams: International Tennis Superstar* (Leading Women). New York, NY: Cavendish Square, 2016.

Lagorio-Chafkin, Christine. *We Are the Nerds: The Birth and Tumultuous Life of Reddit, the Internet's Culture Laboratory*. New York, NY: Hachette Books, 2018.

Mallick, Nita, and Judith Guillermo-Newton. *Tennis: Girls Rocking It* (Title IX Rocks!). New York, NY: Rosen Publishing, 2016.

Ohanian, Alexis. *Without Their Permission: The Story of Reddit and a Blueprint for How to Change the World*. New York, NY: Grand Central Publishing, 2016.

Perritano, John. *Reddit* (Tech 2.0: World-Changing Social Media Companies). Broomall, PA: Mason Crest, 2018.

Pina, Andrew. *Serena Williams: Tennis Ace* (People in the News). New York, NY: Lucent Press, 2017.

Schatz, Kate, and Miriam Klein Stahl. *Rad Women Worldwide: Artists and Athletes, Pirates and

Punks, and Other Revolutionaries Who Shaped History. New York, NY: Clarkson Potter, 2017.

Shoup, Kate. *Serena Williams: International Tennis Superstar* (Leading Women). New York, NY: Cavendish Square, 2017.

Stanmyre, Jackie F. *Althea Gibson and Arthur Ashe: Breaking Down Tennis's Color Barrier* (Game-changing Athletes). New York, NY: Cavendish Square, 2016.

Venus and Serena Williams (Quotes from the Greatest Athletes). New York, NY: AV2 By Weigl, 2017.

Williams, Serena. *My Life: Queen of the Court*. New York, NY: Simon & Schuster, 2010.

BIBLIOGRAPHY

Adams, Tim. "Queen of the Court: An Autobiography by Serena Williams." *Guardian*, September 12, 2009. https://www.theguardian.com/books/2009/sep/13/queen-of-the-court.

Amatulli, Jenna. "Serena Williams Hits Tennis Court in Tutu Amid Catsuit Ban and People Love It." Huffington Post, August 28, 2018. https://www.huffingtonpost.com/entry/serena-williams-hits-tennis-court-in-tutu-amid-catsuit-ban_us_5b8547d4e4b0511db3d1b39a.

Associated Press. "Top-Ranked Serena Williams Withdraws from the Italian Open." Tennis.com, May 14, 2015. http://www.tennis.com/pro-game/2015/05/top-ranked-serena-williams-withdraws-from-italian-open/54891.

Beier, Chris, and Daniel Wolfman. "The Emotional Story of Reddit's Start & Sale." *Inc.*, May 10, 2012. https://www.inc.com/chris-beier-and-daniel-wolfman/alexis-ohanian-reddit-founder-emotional-back-story-start-and-sale.html?cid=readmore.

Bethell, Katy. "Founding, Funding and Fatherhood with Alexis Ohanian." Commonwealth Club, July 25, 2018. https://www.commonwealthclub.org/events/archive/podcast/founding-funding-and-fatherhood-alexis-ohanian.

Bhardwaj, Prachi. "Serena Williams' Husband and Reddit Co-Founder Reveals the Most Important Thing He's Learned from His Wife—and It Holds a Valuable Lesson for Any Power Couple." Business Insider, April 12, 2018. https://www.businessinsider.com/what-reddit-cofounder-alexis-ohanian-learned-from-serena-williams-2018-4.

Bissinger, Buzz. "Serena Williams's Love Match." *Vanity Fair*, August 2017. https://www.vanityfair.com/style/2017/06/serena-williams-cover-story.

Britton, Bianca. "Four Billboards Say Serena Williams Is the 'Greatest Momma of All Time.'" CNN, February 28, 2018. https://www.cnn.com/2018/02/27/tennis/serena-williams-billboard-intl/index.html.

Brown, Laura. "The Number 1." *InStyle*, June 26, 2018. https://www.instyle.com/news/serena-williams-august-cover.

Buckanoff, Marissa. "Tennis Ace Serena Williams Appointed UNICEF's Newest Goodwill Ambassador." UNICEF, September 20, 2011. https://www.unicef.org/malaysia/media_news11-tennis-ace-serena-williams-appointed-unicef-goodwill-ambassador.html.

Cruickshank, Saralyn. "Reddit Co-Founder Alexis Ohanian on Innovation, Entrepreneurship, and Defaulting to 'Yes.'" Hub, April 30, 2018. https://hub.jhu.edu/2018/04/30/alexis-ohanian-reddit-talk-hopkins.

Curtis, Charles. "Alexis Ohanian Wrote Sweetest Message to Serena." *USA Today*, November

BIBLIOGRAPHY

20, 2017. https://www.usatoday.com/story/sports/ftw/2017/11/20/alexis-ohanians-message-to-serena-after-their-wedding-you-are-the-greatest-of-all-time/107879620.

Friedman, Vanessa. "Serena Williams, the U.S. Open, and the Sexist Rules of Fashion and Tennis." *New York Times*, August 28, 2018. https://www.nytimes.com/2018/08/28/style/tennis-fashion-us-open-serena-williams.html.

Gelles, David. "Alexis Ohanian Talks Reddit, Serena Williams and Metallica." *New York Times*, April 4, 2018. https://www.nytimes.com/2018/04/04/business/alexis-ohanian-talks-reddit-serena-williams-and-metallica.html?smid=tw-nytimes&smtyp=cur.

Greenberg, Andy. "How Reddit's Alexis Ohanian Became the Mayor of the Internet." *Forbes*, June 5, 2012. https://www.forbes.com/sites/andygreenberg/2012/06/05/how-reddits-alexis-ohanian-became-the-mayor-of-the-internet/#3c86db35aa15.

Jacobs, Lola. "Serena Williams Talks Family and Motherhood With 'Vogue.'" *Vibe*, January 10, 2018. https://www.vibe.com/2018/01/serena-williams-family-vogue-cover.

Jalili, Candice. "Alexis Ohanian's Quotes About Serena Williams & What He Learned from Her Will Ruin You." Elite Daily, April 4, 2018. https://www.elitedaily.com.

Juneau, Jen. "Serena Williams and Alexis Ohanian Expecting First Child." *People,* April 19, 2017. https://people.com/parents/serena-williams-pregnant-alexis-ohanian-expecting-first-child.

Kimble, Lindsay. "All About Serena Williams and Alexis Ohanian's Romance Leading Up to Their Baby News." *People*, April 19, 2017. https://people.com/sports/serena-williams-alexis-ohanian-romance.

Lagorio-Chafkin, Christine. "A 'Holy Shit' Moment: How Steve Huffman and Alexis Ohanian Built Reddit, the 'Front Page of the Internet.'" *Vanity Fair*, September 24, 2018. https://www.vanityfair.com/news/2018/09/how-steve-huffman-and-alexis-ohanian-built-reddit.

Lagorio-Chafkin, Christine. "How Alexis Ohanian Built a Front Page of the Internet." *Inc.*, May 30, 2012. https://www.inc.com/magazine/201206/christine-lagorio/alexis-ohanian-reddit-how-i-did-it.html.

Macon, Alexandra. "Inside Serena Williams's Fairy-Tale Wedding in New Orleans." *Vogue*, November 17, 2017. https://www.vogue.com/article/serena-williams-wedding-new-orleans.

Maine, D'Arcy. "Alexis Ohanian Shares Hilarious Story About First Date with Serena Williams." ESPN.com, May 9, 2018. http://www.espn.com/espnw/culture/the-buzz/article/23450993/alexis-ohanian-shares-hilarious-story-first-date-serena-williams.

BIBLIOGRAPHY

Nordstrom, Leigh. "Exclusive: Serena Williams Hopes 'S' Means Success." *WWD*, May 30, 2018. https://wwd.com/eye/people/exclusive-serena-williams-launches-serena-line-1202683280.

NPR. *How I Built This*, "Live Episode! Reddit: Alexis Ohanian & Steve Huffman." Released August 31, 2017. https://www.npr.org/2017/10/03/545635014/live-episode-reddit-alexis-ohanian-steve-huffman.

Ohanian, Alexis. "Alexis Ohanian: Congress and Statehouses Need to Develop Better Family Leave Policies." *The Hill*, July 12, 2018. https://thehill.com/opinion/healthcare/396744-alexis-ohanian-congress-and-statehouses-need-to-develop-better-family.

Ohanian, Alexis. "Ararat & Me—One Armenian's Return to the Homeland." Kiva.org. Retrieved October 26, 2018. https://www.kiva.org/blog/ararat-me-one-armenians-return-to-the-homeland.

Ohanian, Alexis. "Reddit Founder on Startup Success: Identify a Genuine Need and Fill It." *Entrepreneur*, October 1, 2013. https://www.entrepreneur.com/article/228535.

Papenfuss, Mary. "Billie Jean King Tells French Open Officials to Stop 'Policing Women's Bodies.'" Huffington Post, August 27, 2018. https://www.huffingtonpost.com/entry/billie-jean-king-french-open-dress-code_us_5b836a68e4b0729515142331.

Paul, Kari. "Reddit Co-founder—and Serena Williams Spouse—Alexis Ohanian on Frugal Living." MarketWatch, September 3, 2018. https://www.marketwatch.com/story/reddit-co-founder-alexis-ohanian-on-frugal-living-and-what-hell-teach-his-daughter-2018-08-14.

Porter, Lauren. "Serena Williams on Finding Love in an Unexpected Place: 'I Never Thought I Would Have Married A White Guy.'" *Essence*, May 2, 2018. https://www.essence.com.

Reed, Sam. "Serena Williams's and Alexis Ohanian's Astrological Signs Usually Fight About This One Thing." *InStyle*, November 12, 2018. https://www.instyle.com.

Rosenbush, Steven, and Steven Norton. "Reddit Co-Founder Alexis Ohanian Steps Aside, Focuses on Initialized Capital." *Wall Street Journal*, February 7, 2018. https://blogs.wsj.com/cio/2018/02/07/reddit-co-founder-alexis-ohanian-steps-aside-focuses-on-initialized-capital.

Shapiro, Mark, Michael Antinoro, and Will Staeger, executive producers. *Being Serena*. DVD. Performance by Serena Williams. HBO Sports, 2018. https://www.hbo.com/being-serena.

Shmerler, Cindy. "Serena Williams Shrugs Off Catsuit Concerns." *New York Times*, August 25, 2018. https://www.nytimes.com/2018/08/25/sports/serena-williams-shrugs-off-catsuit-concerns.html.

Victor, Daniel. "Serena Williams Is GQ's 'Woman' of the Year. Fans Ask: What's with the Quotation

BIBLIOGRAPHY

Marks?" *New York Times*, November 14, 2018. https://www.nytimes.com/2018/11/14/business/media/serena-williams-gq.html.

Wagner, Kurt. "Reddit Raised $200 Million in Funding and Is Now Valued at $1.8 Billion." CNBC, July 31, 2017. https://www.cnbc.com/2017/07/31/reddit-worth-1-point-8-billion.html.

Wenger, Stephanie. "Celebrate Serena Williams and Alexis Ohanian's Wedding Anniversary with a Look Back at Their Sweetest Moments Together." E!News, November 16, 2018. https://www.eonline.com.

Wiedeman, Reeves. "Child's Play." *New Yorker*, June 2, 2014. https://www.newyorker.com/magazine/2014/06/02/childs-play-6.

Williams, Serena (serenawilliams). "I said yes." Reddit post. Retrieved October 26, 2018. https://www.reddit.com/r/isaidyes/comments/5kycyr/i_said_yes.

Williams, Serena (serenawilliams). "My Dearest Baby …" Instagram post, April 24, 2017. https://www.instagram.com/p/BTROccdhdjo/?utm_source=ig_embed.

Williams, Serena. "Serena Williams: What My Life-Threatening Experience Taught Me about Giving Birth." CNN, February 20, 2018. https://www.cnn.com.

Williams, Serena, with Daniel Paisner. *On the Line*. New York, NY: Grand Central Publishing, 2009.

INDEX

A
Aneres clothing line, 19
Armani, Giorgio, 67
Armenian genocide, 26
Australian Open, 16, 18, 53, 55, 56, 59, 82

B
Baynham, Dakota, 53
Being Serena, 64, 71, 74, 76, 83, 84, 89
Berlei, 56
Black Panther catsuit, 85–87
blood clots, 23, 61
Breadpig, 37–38
Brinker, Maureen Connolly, 18

C
Cavalieri Hotel, 40, 52, 53
Clijsters, Kim, 21–22
Coinbase, 80
Compton courts, 12
CompUSA, 27
Condé Nast, 35, 36
Contemporary Arts Center of New Orleans, 65
Court, Margaret, 18, 78

D
Drake, 42

E
Eiffel Tower, 46
Erivo, Cynthia, 71

F
Festival of Media Global, 42
Folgers 1850, 80
French Open, 18, 23, 45, 48, 85

G
Gibson, Althea, 16
Goldstein, Adam, 38
Graf, Steffi, 7, 18, 57

H
Haupt, Zane, 42
Hilfiger, Tommy, 53
Hipmunk, 8, 38
Home Shopping Network, 19, 84
Huffman, Steve, 29–33, 35, 38

I
Indian Wells tennis tournament, 83, 84

INDEX

Initialized Capital, 8, 38, 79, 80, 82, 87
Instacart, 31, 80

J

Jehovah's Witnesses, 12, 50

K

Kerber, Angelique, 55
King, Billie Jean, 87
Kingdom Hall, 12, 14

L

La Ménagerie, 46
Late Show with Stephen Colbert, The, 47

M

Macci, Rick, 14
maternity and paternity leave, 75
McQueen, Alexander, 67
Miller, Anne, 14
Mouratoglou, Patrick, 83
Mubadala World Tennis Championship, 76, 78
My Mobile Menu, 30

N

Navratilova, Martina, 7
New Edition, 71
Nike tennis outfits, 84, 85

O

Ohanian, Alexis
  abandoning hopes of law school, 29
  angel investing, 38
  billboard photos for Serena, 83
  birth, 26
  childhood, 26–27
  early jobs, 27–28
  early love of computer technology, 26–27
  education, 27–29
  fatherhood, 74, 75
  Kiva Fellowship, 37
  marriage, 6–7
  mayor of the internet, 38
  mother's illness, 35–36
  net worth, 80
  Reddit founding, 7–8, 25, 32–33
  speaking engagements, 39
  thirty-second birthday, 49–50
  trip to Armenia, 37
Ohanian, Alexis "Olympia" Jr., 59, 61, 62, 64, 66, 71, 76, 78, 83, 87

109

Ohanian, Anke, 26, 35–36, 66
Ohanian, Christopher, 26, 37
On the Line autobiography, 14, 16, 19, 21
Opendoor, 80
Osaka, Naomi, 88

P
Paid Leave for the US, 75
Price, Yetunde, 10, 18–19, 22
Puma, 17

Q
Queen of the Court, 23

R
racism, 84
Reddit, 32–33, 34–37, 39, 79

S
Safarova, Lucie, 48
Serena and Alexis
  adjusting to parenthood, 72, 74, 76
  birth of daughter, 59
  delivery complications, 61, 64
  engagement announcement, 54
  first date, 45–47
  first meeting, 8, 40–42, 44
  marriage proposal, 53–54
  marriage vows, 68
  media response to their union, 9
  pregnancy, 56–57, 58
  wedding, 65–69, 71–72
Serena clothing line, 85
Serena Slam, 18
Smoller, Jill, 40, 44, 52, 53
start-up companies, 29, 31, 36, 38, 80
Steindorff, Jessica, 40, 42, 55–56
Stukes, Sabriya, 44

T
Tan, Garry, 38

U
University of Virginia, 28–30
US Open, 16, 18, 21, 23, 49, 87, 88

INDEX

V

Versace, 69
Vogt, Val, 66
Vuitton, Louis, 87

W

Wade, Abdoulaye, 21
Wiig, Kristen, 41
William Morris Endeavor Entertainment, 44
Williams, Oracene, 10, 12, 14, 21, 66, 72
Williams, Richard, 10–11, 12, 18
Williams, Serena
  being homeschooled, 14
  birth, 10
  childhood, 10–12, 14
  and fashion design, 17, 19, 69
  fears about motherhood, 59, 64, 71
  Grand Slam titles, 7, 16, 18, 23, 48, 56–57, 78, 88
  GQ "Woman of the Year," 88
  heath problems and injuries, 18, 19, 23, 59, 61
  marriage, 6–7
  move to Florida, 14
  net worth, 84
  Olympic medals, 23
  return to tennis after childbirth, 76
  siblings, 10–11
  trip to West Africa, 21, 24
  turning professional, 14, 16
  UNICEF ambassador, 24, 62
  US Tennis Association probation, 23
  wedding dresses, 67–68, 69
Williams, Venus, 12, 14, 16–17, 18, 22, 55, 57, 59, 83, 84
Wimbledon, 18, 23
Wise, Mike, 72
Without Their Permission: How the 21st Century Will Be Made, Not Managed, 8, 38

Y

Y Combinator, 29, 31, 38

ABOUT THE AUTHOR

Alexis Burling has written numerous books for young readers on a variety of topics ranging from current events and career advice to biographies of famous people, including Aung San Suu Kyi, Robert Boyle, Anne Frank, Harper Lee, and Drake. She is also a book critic, with reviews published in the *New York Times*, *San Francisco Chronicle*, and other prominent publications. She lives with her husband in Portland, Oregon.

PHOTO CREDITS

Cover Mike Pont/WireImage/Getty Images; p. 6 Ian West/AFP/Getty Images; p. 11 Paul Harris/Getty Images; p. 13 Art Seitz/Gamma-Rapho/Getty Images; p. 15 Ken Levine/Getty Images; p. 17 Professional Sport/Popperfoto/Getty Images; p. 20 Gustavo Caballero/Getty Images; p. 26 Seth Poppel/Yearbook Library; p. 28 Robert Llewellyn/Photolibrary/Getty Images; p. 30 Kristoffer Tripplaar/Sipa USA/AP Images; p. 32 Bloomberg/Getty Images; p. 36 © AP Photo; p. 41 S.Borisov/Shutterstock.com; p. 43 Ian Walton/Getty Images; p. 46 Guilhem Vellut/Flickr/Ménagerie (Zoo) @ Jardin des Plantes @ Paris/CC BY 2.0; p. 48 Clive Brunskill/Getty Images; pp. 52, 60 Karwai Tang/WireImage/Getty Images; p. 55 David Livingston/Getty Images; p. 57 Icon Sportswire/Getty Images; p. 63 Richard Shiro/Getty Images; p. 67 csfotoimages/iStock Editorial/Getty Images; p. 70 Johnny Nunez/WireImage/Getty Images; p. 73 NPA/Jonathan Rebboah/News Pictures/WENN/Newscom; p. 77 Nezar Balout/AFP/Getty Images; p. 81 Mike Coppola/Getty Images; p. 82 Eugene Gologursky/Getty Images; p. 86 Jean Catuffe/Getty Images; p. 88 Julian Finney/Getty Images; additional interior pages design elements Levchenko Ilia/Shutterstock.com (light streaks), Shmizla/Shutterstock.com (dot pattern), Romeo Budai/EyeEm/Getty Images (sparkle backgrounds).

Design and Layout: Nicole Russo-Duca; Senior Editor: Kathy Kuhtz Campbell; Photo Researcher: Sherri Jackson